Opening up Promises

There is a Hebrew proverb that says 'promise little and do much'. The words of a promise are easy to say, but the promises themselves may be hard to keep. Exploring what people promise, why, and the impact of these promises with children, can help them begin to understand why promises can be so important for believers in God. They can also begin to see the importance of integrity, matching their own words and deeds. Promises – and indeed the 'double strength promise' of a vow – are important to religious believers and are particularly relevant in rites of passage such as baby welcoming and marriage. Also important is the promise of God to human beings shown to religious believers through sacred text, sacred story and their own experience of God.

This curriculum book explores a series of examples of learning about and from promises that are relevant for 4–11 year olds. The units focus on how religion and belief communities use promises at significant moments of life, how keeping a promise changes behaviour and the presence of promises in sacred text.

The unit for 4–6 year olds uses active learning to think deeply about promises, using the story of the two brothers in the vineyard from the New Testament. For 5–7 year olds we ensure that the much-used story of Noah keeps the focus on the promises of God, the true meaning of the story for Jews and Christians. For 7–9s we explore caring as a response to teaching about promises in Christianity and Sikhism.

Baptism and marriage are two occasions when many people find themselves making promises to their child, one another, the community – and for many people making those promises to God and before God. Baptism is explored with an engaging resource of a series of photos of Abi's baptism; and marriage vows in Judaism, Hinduism and Christianity are explored in an enquiry-style unit of work for 9–11s.

As this is the last book in the 'Opening up . . .' series we have provided a series overview for the subject leader. The next series will begin with *RE Ideas: God*.

Fiona Moss
Editor

Web links: RE Today website

The RE Today website offers subscribers some free additional resources and classroom-ready materials related to this publication. Look out for the 'RE Today on the web' logo at the end of selected articles.

To access resources:

- go to the RE Today website www.retoday.org.uk
- click on the **download login** button and use the password from this term's issue of *REtoday* magazine
- click on **Primary curriculum publication – web supplement**
- click on the title of the publication and scroll down the page to find what you are looking for.

Age focus	Contents	Page
4–6	**Promises, promises** Stephen Pett	2–7
5–7	**Why did God send a rainbow?** Lat Blaylock	8–13
7–9	**Caring for others: how do some people help?** Stephen Pett	14–19
7–11	**What do Christians promise when they welcome a baby?** Lat Blaylock	20–24
9–11	**Why do people make marriage vows?** Fiona Moss	25–31
Subject leader	**Opening Up RE: What the series contains** Rosemary Rivett	32–33

RE Today Services

Promises, promises

4–6

For the teacher

People make lots of promises. The words are easy to say, but the promises themselves may be hard to keep. Exploring what people promise, why, and the impact of these promises, with young children can help them begin to understand why the promises can be so important for believers in God. They can also begin to see the importance of integrity, matching their own words and deeds. These are difficult lessons to grasp fully with 4–6s, but part of an ongoing journey of virtue and right living.

This unit offers six activities to explore promises with children. Ideas for active learning will help children think deeply, using one of Jesus' stories as a stimulus. Some details have been included for the teacher, as background to this story and to help when answering children's questions. Activity 5 supports children's development of the ability to interpret stories. Children then have a chance to come up with a class poem and some actions for themselves.

Activity 1
Getting started

Talk about what a promise is. It's when someone says they are going to do (or not do) something, and then try to make sure that they do it.

Have children made any promises? What are they? *(e.g. I promise to listen to the teacher, to look after my friends, to help my mum, not to trip someone up in the queue).*

Why do we make promises? How do we feel if we break a promise? Or if someone else breaks a promise they made to us?

You might illustrate this with the classic trust game: stand behind a child and ask her to fall backwards – after you promise to catch her . . . !

Promises are about trust. How would the child feel if you broke your promise about catching her? (Please don't!)

What can children do as a result of this unit?

This article supports children working within the Early Learning goals outlined below, and the pupil friendly 'I can . . .' statements for level 1 and 2 describe what older or more able pupils may achieve through this work.

Early Learning goals	I can . . . • listen to what other children in the class say • listen to stories and guess what is going to happen **(listening and attending)** answer questions about the story and about promises **(understanding)** • talk about what happens when someone breaks a promise **(self-confidence and self-awareness)** • show my ideas in drama and stories **(being imaginative)**
Level 1	• **tell the story** Jesus told about the Two Sons • **talk about** which one did right and why
Level 2	• use the story of the Two Sons to say what Jesus thinks about keeping promises • *say why keeping promises is a good thing for others and for me.*

The following resources are available for subscribers to download from the RE Today website:

- A simple PowerPoint sequence to support the learning in this unit
- A copy of the resource sheets on pages 4 and 5 to download

See: www.retoday.org.uk/supplements

Activity 2
Easy peasy!

This simple 'human bar chart' activity helps children to think about different kinds of promises.

Set up four stations in the room by sticking four pieces of A3 paper to the wall or hanging them from the ceiling. The four pieces should say Easy! Quite hard, Very hard, Impossible!!

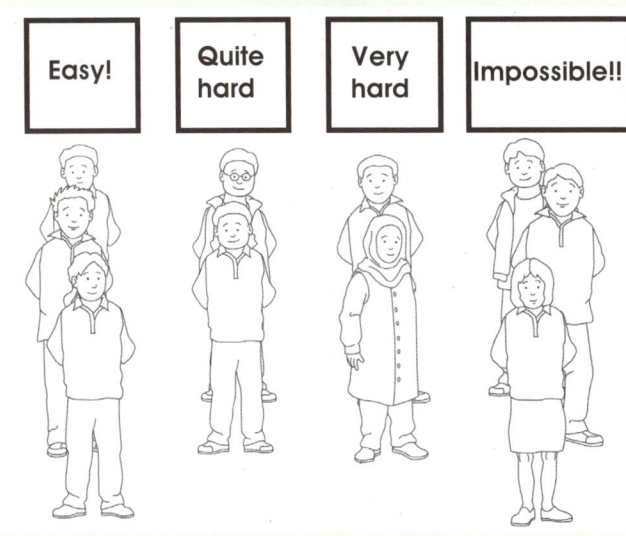

Read out one of the promises below. Ask children if they think this is a promise that is easy, quite hard, very hard or impossible to keep.

Ask them to go and stand by the poster that matches their idea.

For each one, talk about children's choices.

Why do they think they are easy/difficult?

Are there some kinds of promises that are literally impossible to keep, and some that are possible but very hard?

What are the differences between them? (You can't make yourself taller but you could put effort into working very hard.)

Any promises that suggest the ultimate – all, always, never again – are likely to be impossible for human beings to manage!

I promise . . .
- to eat a big bar of chocolate
- to eat a plateful of sprouts at Christmas
- to be the tallest person in the class
- to be the fastest person in the world at 100m
- never to be naughty ever again
- always to be nice to my brother/sister
- to do all the cleaning at home
- to work very hard every day
- to give some of my pocket money to Children in Need or Christian Aid Week
- to give all my money and toys away to charity

Activity 3
Who promises?

Make copies of the cards on page 4, enough to give sets of cards to groups of children in your class. (Copies of the cards are available online to subscribers, to use on an interactive whiteboard.) Give out the pictures first. Talk about what these people do and ask children to think about what promises they might make. Why might these promises be made?

Readers could match the word cards with the correct image. For other children, read out the word cards and ask them to identify and hold up the picture that matches the words.

Talk about the promises. Why are they important? Who are the promises made to? How does it help if people make promises to each other? Who are they made for?

The scout and guide movement emphasise that duty to 'God' refers to God as understood by all religions. The organisations are currently consulting on the idea of a promise for those without a faith.

Activity 4
The Two Sons

Show the children the pictures on page 5 and ask them to think what the story might be.

Tell the children the story from Matthew's Gospel 21:28-32 (see page 5).

Ask them to identify which picture belongs to which part of the story.

> What did the father ask his sons?
>
> How did the first son answer? What did he do?
>
> What did the second son say? What did he do? What title would they give the story? Why?
>
> What promises are made?
>
> Is there a goodie and a baddie? Who are they? Are they goodies and baddies all the way through or is there a turning point? When is that?
>
> Why do they think Jesus told this story?
>
> Who was he talking to and what were they doing?
>
> Is there a moral to this story? What do children think it is?

Ask children to act out the story in groups of three. Ask them to think about how each person in the story would feel. Get one group to act the story out in front of the rest of the class. Stop them at different points and ask what they are thinking and feeling.

More activities to explore Christian understandings of this story can be found on page 6.

RE Today Services

Activity 3   Who promises?

Match the picture and the promise.

I promise to do my best, to love God and to be kind and helpful.	
I promise to help ill people get better.	
I promise to serve the Queen, treat people with respect, and keep the peace.	
I promise to look after this baby and bring her up as a Christian.	
I promise to love you and to stay with you.	

The Two Sons

The parable of the Two Sons – Matthew 21:28-32 (Good News Bible)

[Jesus was talking to the chief priests and leaders.]

'Now, what do you think? There was once a man who had two sons. He went to the older one and said, "Son, go and work in the vineyard today." "I don't want to," he answered, but later he changed his mind and went. Then the father went to the other son and said the same thing. "Yes, sir," he answered, but he did not go. Which one of the two did what his father wanted?'

'The older one,' they answered.

RE Today Services

© 2013 RE Today Services
Permission is granted to photocopy this page for use in classroom activities in schools that have purchased this publication.

5

Information file: for the teacher

Lessons for Christians from the parable of the Two Sons (Matthew 21)

This information will help prepare you for Activity 5 by explaining how Christians understand this story.

Jesus is talking to chief priests and elders in the temple courts in his last week in Jerusalem. They are challenging his authority. He ends his story by challenging the leaders: they criticise others and 'talk the talk' but don't 'walk the walk'.

The last two verses say:

So Jesus said to them, 'I tell you: the tax collectors and sinners are going into the Kingdom of God ahead of you. For John the Baptist came to you showing you the right path to take, and you would not believe him; but the tax collectors and sinners believed him. Even when you saw this, you did not later change your minds and believe him.'

Christians don't all agree about the meaning of this story but the lessons might go something like this:

- The father is like God, and asks human beings to follow his commands.
- No 1 son is like those people who rebel against God, but then realise that they are wrong, and so turn back and follow his commands. This pleases God.
- No 2 son is like those people who promise that they will follow God's commands, but don't. They think they are OK, but God is not pleased with them.

From this, it seems that Jesus would say it is better to be No 1 son. The No 2 son might not be happy with that, but Jesus is firm about this. Some people (like the chief priests that Jesus is talking to) think they are OK and pleasing God, but they aren't really.

You might compare this story with the story of the Lost Sheep, where the shepherd represents God. Or the story of the Lost Son, where the father represents God, as he does in this story. This will help children to realise that characters in some of Jesus' parables represent God or religious leaders or sinful people, for example.

Activity 5
Interpreting: suggesting meanings

Getting across what this story means to Christians is difficult, but this activity will help.

Select some of the following seven sentences, as appropriate to your children (make sure you include the last one). Put them on cards for readers, or read them out one at a time to the class. Talk about what they mean. Ask them to choose which ones might be the message of the story for Christians. They are not all good lessons from the story!

- Always eat your vegetables.
- Actions speak louder than words!
- God is happy if you break your promises to him.
- Obey your parents!
- As long as you clean your teeth, God is pleased with you.
- It's no good just talking about helping others, you actually have to do it.
- If you say you love God, you need to show it in how you treat other people.

Some of these messages are important for anyone. Make sure you also talk about how important the last one is for Christians. Christians should try to show their love for God by following his commands.

Activity 6
Promise poems

a Ask children to come up with some impossible promises – the wilder the better! Record their ideas, in writing or on an audio recorder. Promises to do with, for example: *school; home; next Sunday; their family; friends; something they will say; when they are grown up; their town; the world; and, where appropriate, God.*

Next, ask the children to think of things they might really promise to do with some or all of these.

Gather the wild impossible promises together and weave in the real promises. Create a class poem for display, like this, using the frame on page 7.

b Are there any promises children might make about how they treat each other in your school? Can you record these on your display? Might you come back to those every now and again and talk about them? One lesson from Jesus' story is that it is important that these are not just words but are also matched with actions.

Class promises!

We **could** promise to **fly like Superman!**

We **do** promise not to give up when things are difficult.

We **could** promise to be **the best pupils who have ever lived!**

We **do** promise to try our best…

We **could** promise to…

We **do** promise to…

We **could** promise to…

We **do** promise to…

We **could** promise to…

We **do** promise to…

WHY DID GOD SEND A RAINBOW?

5–7

For the teacher

This section of the book uses the story of Noah. It can be a touchstone for 'bad RE' – the class theme is water, so we do Noah. The class theme is transport: we do Noah (it has a boat!). Two times table, anyone? But the story is rich, and everlastingly retold. Noah is revered in Judaism, Christianity and Islam. So here are five activities to enable 5–7 year olds to enjoy the story together, and think for themselves carefully about safety and danger in the story, and why some people trust in God's promises.

Storytelling is the foundation of these learning ideas. Teachers will do this best if they search for the storyteller within, and refresh their understanding of the story by reading it in Genesis 6–9, then telling it in the best way they can think of. Alternatives would be to use DVD (Testament, Channel 4 Learning, is good), or read the story aloud from one of the many available books.

There are three fun, team activities, which can be used throughout the teaching of the story. They are all fun, and they will be used by the good teacher to make links to the story.

There are five learning activities that go with the story and the fun. Plan your lessons to use the ones you like most, those that will help your children make connections.

What can children do as a result of this unit?

The following pupil-friendly 'I can' statements describe the learning that may be expected of pupils in the 5–7 age range. Pupils don't have to do them all, just show they can do some of them.

Level	Description of achievement: I can . . .
1	• **recount** the outline of the story simply • *talk about* how Noah felt at different points in the story (SEAL link).
2	• **identify** one thing that Noah might have hoped for when he came out of the ark • **suggest a meaning** for the rainbow, the dove or the olive leaf in the story • *say sensitively* what I think about my own hopes for the future.
3	• **describe** several examples of what Noah might have hoped for when he came out of the ark. • **make a link** between the Noah story and my own hopes for the future. • *ask some questions* about the story, its symbols and its meaning.

Curriculum links

Noah and literacy: This is a traditional story, and a story from another culture. Pupils and teachers will get great learning value out of this story if some Literacy time is spent unpacking the text.

Noah in another sacred text – the holy Qur'an: You might point out to the pupils that Muslim people revere Noah (the Prophet Nuh in Islam) as well. A version of his story is found the Qur'an, and is often told to Muslim children.

A story about God: Hamlet without the prince would be mildly odd, but Noah without God is a travesty. God is clearly the lead character in the Noah 'novella'. Yet the story is often told in primary versions without God in it at all. So why call it RE then? Teaching should let the story be what it is in faith terms, and should enable pupils to explore their own questions and ideas about God.

Fixed and fluid: Religious stories are often fixed in text, but never fixed in interpretation. So if you (or the pupils) ask: 'Why would God do that?' or 'Is it fair?', or 'What does this mean?' then they become interpreters. That's what is supposed to happen.

Let the questions flourish.

Sophie, 8, from Naseby Primary School, made this lovely collage of the story.

RE Today Services

Three fun activities about the story of Noah and the ark

Card ark!

This is really a design activity! Give children in teams of five or six some old cardboard boxes, scissors and masking tape and some big felt-tip pens. Remind them that God asked Noah to build an ark before the floods came. Can they build a card ark in 20 minutes? Tell them that they will need co-operation to do it!

When the groups have each made their ark (and they will probably need an extension of time!), they can draw portholes, and even make some animals to go on deck (playdough?).

This is a lot of fun, and teachers should plan to use the team experience in telling the Noah story during the learning activities.

Night-time feeding on the ark: a blindfold game

Choose two children to be Mr and Mrs Noah. All other children are in pairs. Tell the children that Mr and Mrs Noah (blindfolded) will bring food to their animals at night time, but because it is dark they cannot see which animals are which. What to feed each animal?

Give each pair a card with an animal on it (word or picture). This list might do: cows, dogs, cats, monkeys, horses, elephants, mice, parrots, chickens, lions, bears, frogs, sheep, pigeons, crows. Add some more difficult ones if you like!

When the children have had time to think the game starts: teacher says 'Feeding time' and all the 'animals' make their noises. If Mr and Mrs Noah can identify them, they get a point.

It should get easier as, when identified, those 'animals' are quiet. If it's too confusing a sound, get them to make their noises one at a time. Several pairs will want a turn at Mr and Mrs Noah.

Ask the children why do Jewish and Christian people think God wanted to save the animals?

A rainbow of seven promises

Tell the class that Christian and Jewish people believe God has made some promises to humanity, like the one he made to Noah at the end of the story. Write these onto large 'arcs' of card or paper with a big pen. Christians and Jews believe that God promises to:

- Never go to sleep (Gods sees everything)
- Love humans always
- Bring fruit when we plant seeds
- Give us a mixture of rain and sunshine
- Forgive us if we are truly sorry
- Listen to our prayers
- Never leave us alone
- Give us calm hearts if we pray
- Save us from evil.

Talk about which promise is most useful, helpful, interesting, inspiring or unbelievable.

Can pupils suggest which promise is which colour – red, orange, yellow, green, blue, indigo, violet? Why? This conversation is about symbolism, and children usually have interesting ideas.

Can pupils suggest a moment in the story where Noah might have been glad of each promise? Which seven promises do the class like best, and which two will they not include in their rainbow?

In small groups, get pupils to collage one of the promises onto a stripe of a rainbow, and put them all together to make a rainbow of seven colours.

Learning activities about Noah and the promise of God

Activity 1
God's promise: the story of Noah and the ark

Pupils may have heard this story already, but make the telling exciting! Tell the story in a fresh and exciting way: the DVD *Testament: The Bible in Animation* (1997 – still available) works well.

Alternatively, gather several 'Noah' storybooks for 2–5 year olds and ask pupils to look at them and compare the story they tell with the one in the Bible itself (extracts from Genesis 6–9 could be used). This is a popular story for small children, but there is more to it as well!

Ask pairs of pupils to do a version of the story in 10 sentences on sticky notes, then swap with another pair and sort and order the other pair's sentences.

Activity 2
Noah in 30 sentences and 30 pictures

This is a great way to get the whole class involved in retelling the story creatively. Use the sentences on page 12, blown up to A3 and cut up. There are 30, which is a magic number in education: the number of children in a class.

Tell the children we are going to make a class art gallery or artbook of the whole story, and everyone is going to do a different bit of the story.

Differentiate by giving harder sentences to those better able to respond.

Ask children to talk before they start, within a small group, about the different ways they could do their drawing.

Give time, good quality art resources and conversational support to help children do a picture to be proud of. When they are all done, sequence them. This can make a good class book, or a display as an art gallery. A nice feature for a parents evening – or an inspector's visit!

Activity 3
Responding to the story: five key moments for Noah's prayers

Ask pupils to think about the five key moments in the story.

- What is a key moment?
- What were the key moments here?

These might include:

1. When God first spoke to Noah
2. When Noah got the last pair of animals inside the ark and the rain started.
3. When Noah prayed for God to keep them all safe
4. When Noah's dove brought the leaf back to the ark
5. When the ark door was opened and the promise came with the rainbow.

For younger pupils, show them five prayers Noah might have said (see page 13 below).

Can they discuss the prayers and put them in the right order?

For older ones with writing skills, ask them to write five simple prayers that Noah might have said at each of the key moments. Give this activity in pairs with learning partners.

Talk about the Christian belief that God hears and answers people's prayers.

- Does prayer make a difference?
- What thoughts do the children have about praying?

RE Today Services

Learning activities about Noah and the promise of God

Activity 4
Making up good questions – what is the Noah story all about?

You could put three articulate children in 'hot seats' for this, and ask them to have a go at these questions in turn. Ask them to try and give a reason for their answers. You could give these questions to other pupils to read out, then get all the children to make up more deep questions about Noah's story.

The story suggests answers to these kinds of questions. Have a 'Philosophy for Children' type enquiry into one of the questions. Get pupils to think about the answers to these questions both in the story and in their own thinking. Teach the class that religious stories sometimes last thousands of years and are loved by millions of people because they suggest answers to big questions.

When was Noah safe in the story?	Was it fair of God to send the flood?	Will there ever be another flood?	Can people make a difference to the world?
What is the most dangerous moment in the story?	Do animals matter to God?	Is goodness rewarded in life?	Does God keep his promises?

The God of second chances: the story of Noah

When people turn away from God, our only Master
Nothing good happens: it can lead to disaster.
In Noah's time the wickedness grew faster than it oughta
God sent a flood to end it all: a clean up with some water.

The animals were saved by God with a bit of Noah's help,
They went into the ark with honks and roars and yelps.
Forty days of rain, and a dove with a leaf,
They came out to a fresh, clean world full of relief.

God saved the grumpy camel and the coloured butterfly
God saved the muddy pig and the birds that flutter by,
God saved the hippo, the rabbit and gnu,
God loved to save things including you.

Humans we are stupid, and sometimes we are bad;
We don't deserve the chances and the kindness that we've had.
But when you make a mess up, if your life goes askew
The God of second chances will come and rescue you.

Activity 5
Poetry and meanings

Share the poem with the class. Could two children read it out – alternate verses? If it is too hard, get some 9 or 10 year olds to come and read it well to your class.

Talk about the meaning of the poem and the idea that God is 'the god of second chances'.

- Why do Christians and Jews say God is 'the God of second chances'?
- Do you agree with this idea? If you make a mistake, can God rescue you?

The story of Noah in 30 bites

Once upon a time there was an old man called Noah.	Noah gave his boat a name. It was called 'The Ark'.	After ages in the water, the ark bumped down on a mountain.
Noah loved God, and tried to live kindly, but everyone else seemed to be selfish.	At last, all the animals were inside the ark and the mighty doors closed.	Slowly the water drained away, and the grass grew back.
God spoke to Noah: There will be a great flood! Build a great boat to escape!	The rain began to fall. It fell more and more heavily. The earth began to flood.	At last God told Noah to open the door of the ark, and all the animals ran free.
Noah and his children built a huge boat on dry land out of planks of wood.	The rain kept on falling hard and splashing into the floods. The ark floated away.	Noah and his family said 'thank you' prayers to God for their safety through the flood.
God said to Noah: 'Get two of every animal into the boat!'	Huge black rainclouds poured water down in buckets. The whole earth flooded.	In the sky behind the ark a rainbow appeared. It was seven beautiful colours.
Everyone who saw Noah building his boat thought he was crazy! Noah trusted God.	The ark floated on the water like a little boat. Noah and the animals were safe inside.	God promised Noah: the rainbow is a sign that the earth will never flood like that again.
Noah got the animals to come into his boat two by two.	After the rain stopped, the ark still floated. Noah prayed to God: 'Will we ever get out?'	The story of Noah is a warning to us not to be too selfish or greedy.
The elephants were very big. The camels were very grumpy.	God told Noah to choose a dove, and send her out. She flew away.	The story of Noah says that it's good to trust God. Jews and Christians believe this.
The tigers were very scary. The monkeys were very naughty.	Noah wondered if the dove would ever come back. He kept a lookout.	The rainbow is a sign of God's promises: plant seeds, and fruit will grow.
The rabbits were very sweet. The pandas were very cuddly.	Noah's dove flew back with a leaf in her beak. Then he knew things were growing again.	Some people always thank God when they see the rainbow.

© 2013 RE Today Services
Permission is granted to photocopy this page for use in classroom activities in schools that have purchased this publication.

Noah's prayers

Here are five prayers that Noah might have said. What is the right order for them?

- Dear God, please help me to collect all the animals. I don't want to forget any!

- Dear God ~ Thank you for the chance to save every animal on earth. Sorry so many people have been greedy and selfish!

- Dear God ~ Thank you for the beautiful rainbow and for your promise never to flood the earth again!

- Dear God ~ Keep us all safe inside the ark. As the rain falls from the clouds, keep us hopeful about the future!

- Dear God ~ Bless this dove. When she flies out, please may she find food and please may she return safe!

RE Today Services

© 2013 RE Today Services
Permission is granted to photocopy this page for use in classroom activities in schools that have purchased this publication.

Caring for others: how do some people help?

7–9

For the teacher

Jesus summed up his teachings in two phrases: love God and love your neighbour (Matthew 22:34-40). Sikhs believe that the path to God is found by meditating on God (*nam japna*), working hard (*kirat karna*) and sharing with others (*vand chakna*).

This unit explores the ways in which some Christians and Sikhs respond to these commands. Many of them see people suffering from poverty, or in the wake of an international disaster, and they are determined to help. The activities on the following pages help pupils to think about the kinds of promises believers might make in order to show their love for God and for others, and the actions they take as a result.

Of course, it is not only religious believers who show care and concern for the poor, and this unit will encourage pupils to think about whether they are in a position to promise to care for others. It may start you thinking about some actions that your classes might take. If you are not teaching Sikhism, this unit will work with a focus on Christianity alone.

See also

The following are links to web resources from the religious organisations and charities featured in this unit.

Toilet Twinning
See: www.toilettwinning.org

Khalsa Aid
See: www.khalsaaid.org/Snowdon_Walk2012.html
www.khalsaaid.org/2010_Volunteers.html
www.skydiving.co.uk/news2011-10thJuly-KhalsaAid

Cambray Baptist Church football match
See: http://tinyurl.com/brzjyl2
www.youtube.com/watch?v=1E5vUDf9TpU

Manni Kaur
See: http://tinyurl.com/ce3y6j6

Christian Aid week
See: http://tinyurl.com/cvazs7p
www.micahchallenge.org.uk/

What can children do as a result of this unit?

The following pupil-friendly 'I can' statements describe the learning that may be expected of pupils in the 7–9 age range.

	Description of achievement: I can...
2	• **say why** Christians and Sikhs try to help other people • **talk about** how I show that other people matter to me.
3	• **describe** what a Christian and/or a Sikh might do to show that they love God • **make links between** how I help others and how some Christians and/or Sikhs do this.
4	• **show that I understand** how loving God can make a real difference to how some people live • **compare my own ideas** about helping others with Christian and Sikh ideas.

Activity 1
Which would you promise?

Introduce pupils to the idea that making promises can be demanding. If you promise to do (or not to do) something, it can have a cost. This fun activity can get pupils to consider which promises cost more. It serves as a starting point for exploring the kinds of promises people might make to help others, whether religious believers or not.

Ask pupils to decide:
To help a friend in need, which, if any, would you be prepared to promise...?

- to give your lunch money or a packet of sweets?
- to give a packet of crisps or a chocolate bar?
- to give a teddy bear or an hour of TV?
- to give your favourite toy or a week of TV?
- to give a ticket to a One Direction concert or a ticket to a live recording of *The X Factor* [substitute as appropriate to your class!]?
- to give your hair or your teeth?!

Talk about how helping someone might be costly. How much are pupils prepared to give to a friend and how do they decide? Would they promise to help someone? *Why* do people give in order to help others?

RE Today Services

Activity 2
Promises to God

Explain to pupils these key teachings of Jesus and of Guru Nanak.

For **Christians**, the heart of Jesus' teaching is summed up in the verse: 'Love God with all your heart, soul, mind and strength, and love your neighbour as you love yourself.'

For **Sikhs**, the heart of Guru Nanak's teaching is to meditate on God (*nam japna*), work hard (*kirat karna*) and share with others (*vand chakna*).

Ask pupils what believers might promise to do in response to those commands. For example, some may say they will pray and praise God, some may say they will try to follow these commands, or help people who are in trouble. Talk about why believers might promise these things.

Using the information on page 16, look at ways in which some Christians and Sikhs have tried to put their promises to God into action. Websites give more information, with the Toilet Twinning page being the most interactive. Talk about how these actions show the believers' love for God and for others.

Ask pupils to decide how far they would go to help people in need. Would they go as far as the people in these examples?

Activity 4
A story

Page 18 gives one of Jesus' stories, which takes the ideas explored on page 17 a little further.

- Read the story with the children.
- Show them the picture from Mafa.
- Ask eleven of them to pose as the characters in the picture (one is the baby! one is walking past in the courtyard outside; the man in red on the right is Jesus with his disciples).
- Set up a tableau and then get the rest of the children to ask questions. Children 'in the picture' should try and answer.

Talk about what Jesus might have meant about the poor widow giving more than the rich people. Who shows the most love for God and for others?

Are there any implications for pupils? They are young and have limited money, presumably – but can they make as big a gesture as the widow in the story?

Activity 3
Which actions will have most impact?

Page 17 gives eight examples of ways in which people try to help those in need. Some of them do this to serve God and show their concern for others; some people do it because they believe that we should always care for our fellow human beings, without any belief in God.

You might try several activities with this material.

a Give each card to a small group. Get them to read the card and talk together, then explain it to the rest of the class.

b Sort the cards into different groups (pupils can decide the groupings, such as Christian, Sikh, other; or short term/long term; or hidden/public).

c Choose the three that they think will have most impact on helping those in need, and say why.

d Go back to the commands/teachings from Christianity and Sikhism (see Activity 2). Talk about how the actions on the cards fulfil these commands.

Activity 5
How much would you give?

Give your pupils some of the following information:

18% of the world do not have clean, safe drinking water.

14% of the world are hungry or malnourished.

12% cannot read.

(Source: www.miniature-earth.com)

Set up the following situation for pupils:

- You win a prize at a school fair!
- You have just had your birthday, and had lots of great presents.
- Now you unexpectedly have an extra £100.
- You have to decide how to spend it.

On page 19 are some things the pupils could spend their money on. In pairs, ask them to decide how they might spend the £100.

They should explain why they are using the money like this.

See: www.christianaid.org.uk/give/other/presentaid.aspx

How do people show they care for others?

Twin your toilet!

When did you last use the toilet? Did you wash your hands? Imagine having no toilets or running water – imagine having to use the side of the road to go to the toilet . . .

40% of the world's population (2.6 billion people!) don't have somewhere safe, clean and hygienic to go to the loo. The impact of this is that nearly one in five child deaths each year is due to diarrhoea.

Toilet Twinning is part of Tearfund, a Christian organisation. They ask you to pay £60 to twin your toilet with one in a part of the world where people desperately need good toilets – without them, diseases spread and many people die young. For people in poor communities, a hole in the ground is quite literally a life saver.

Help them flush away poverty! You can get a certificate for your loo, and find your twinned toilet on GoogleEarth!

Climb a mountain!

Each year, a group of Sikhs support Khalsa Aid by doing a sponsored walk up Mount Snowdon, the second highest mountain in the UK.

They get sponsorship to raise money which is then used in projects like digging wells to provide clean water in Kenya, or helping the survivors of the earthquake in Haiti in 2010.

This is really important: the newspapers and TV cameras move on to the next big disaster, but recovering from such a huge event like an earthquake can take many years.

Skydive!

Some of the more daring supporters of Khalsa Aid took part in a record-breaking attempt at skydiving, in summer 2012. One hundred and thirty-eight people jumped in tandem – in pairs of one instructor and one volunteer – beating the world record for charity tandem jumping in 24 hours!

Organiser Manpreet Kaur said, 'Khalsa Aid is run by Sikh volunteers and based on the Sikh principles of selfless service and universal love, but the work carried out is for all of humanity. The actual sky dive itself was breath-taking – literally! It was such a unique experience. A great big thank you to those who took part!'

The world's longest football match?

Footballers from Cambray Baptist Church, Cheltenham, and their friends attempted the world record for the longest ever football match, in order to raise money to build a school for Dalit children in India.

They played for 35 hours, including over 15 hours of continuous rain, and the score was 333 (All Stars) to 293 (Cambray FC). They raised £42,000 to build the school.

Jennifer (20) took a year out after school and before university. She spent the time working in southern India.

'I believe that we are all born equal and in the image of God. Everybody has the right to enough food, clean water and a place to call home.'

Sara (17) does five hours every two weeks as a volunteer in her local Cancer Research shop. She sorts out donations and serves customers.

'I think it's really important to help – it's only a few hours of my time but it can make a real difference to the charity.'

Luka (8) watches the 'Children in Need' programme with his parents. Together they phone up to pledge some money. Luka gives part of his pocket money.

'I get upset when I see children living in dirty places. I live in a really nice house. I want to help.'

Manni (30) travelled to Amritsar, India, to work with children with learning difficulties at Pingalwara, a Sikh centre for the poor. On her first visit, Manni spent six months serving God.

'Guru Nanak taught us: "In that place where the lowly are cared for, there the blessings of God's grace rain down."'

Lauren delivers Christian Aid envelopes with her Nan each year, and then goes back to collect people's gifts. Lauren (10) says:

'Most people are happy to give some money. Last year we collected over £130 on our street! That will make a real difference!'

Tim (46) works for Micah Challenge UK.

'The Bible says that God wants us to live like this – "To act fairly, love mercy, and to walk humbly with your God" (Micah 6:8). At work we try to put that into action by getting governments to do everything they can to help the poorest people in the world.'

Jo and her husband Phil **tithe** their earnings. This means they give 10% of the money they earn every month. They give some of the money to their church and some to people they know who are struggling.

'The Bible talks about giving the first part of what you have to God, not leaving God till last.' says Jo. *'It helps us not to be greedy.'*

Harvinder (13) doesn't have much of his own money. He does help his granddad, though. Grandad can't see very well, so Harvinder reads books to him for a few hours each week.

'I love my Grandad and he's done a lot for me and my family. I want to do something for him too.'

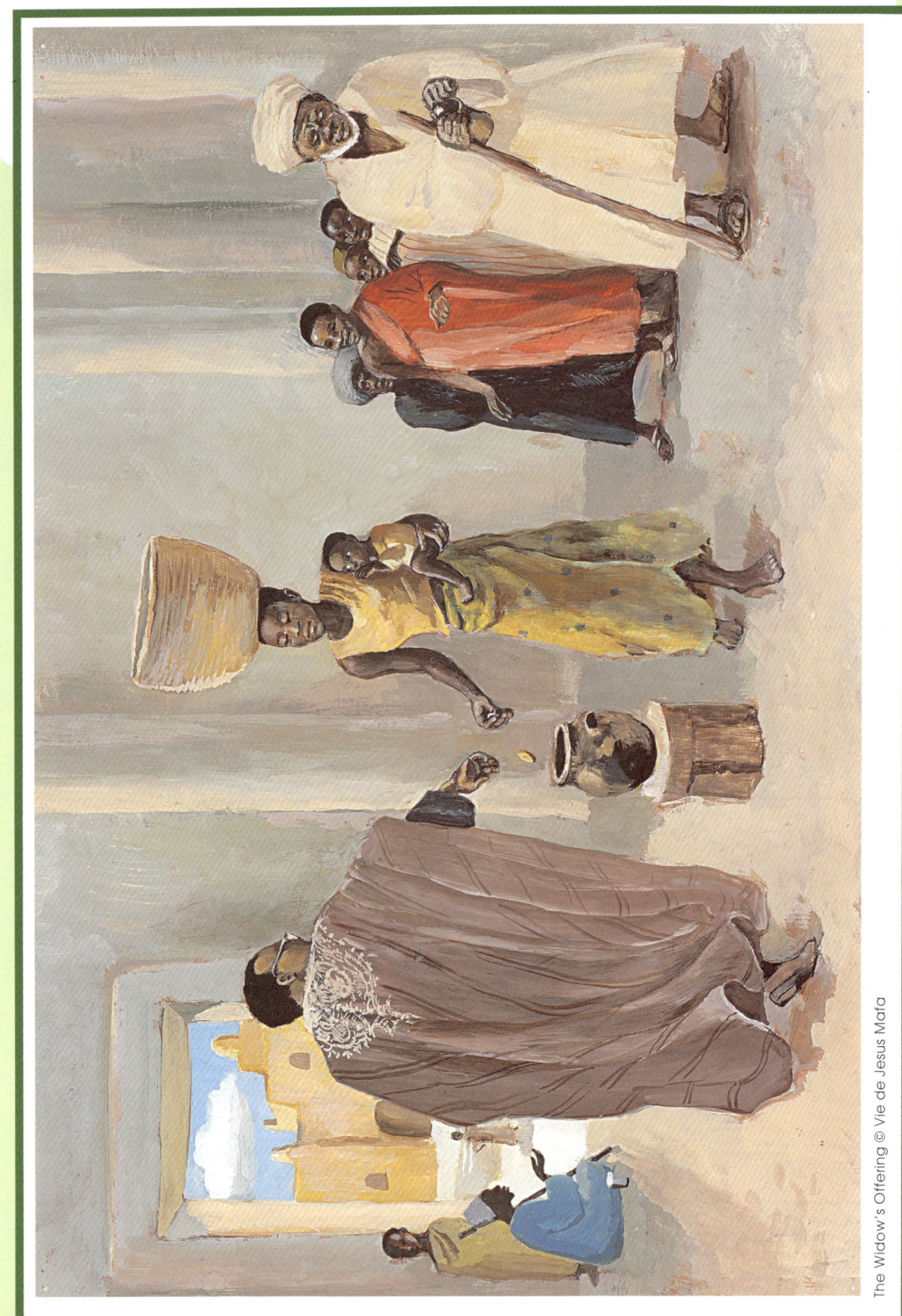

The Widow's Offering: a story from Christianity

As Jesus sat near the Temple treasury, he watched the people as they dropped in their money. Many rich men dropped in a lot of money; then a poor widow came along and dropped in two little copper coins, worth about a penny. He called his disciples together and said to them, 'I tell you that this poor widow put more in the offering box than all the others. For the others put in what they had to spare of their riches; but she, poor as she is, put in all she had – she gave all she had to live on.'

Good News Bible,
Mark 12:41-44

This picture is also available for subscribers to download to show on the whiteboard.

See: www.retoday.org.uk

The Widow's Offering © Vie de Jesus Mafa

This image is available for subscribers to download from the REToday website

See: www.retoday.org.uk/supplements

© 2013 RE Today Services
Permission is granted to photocopy this page for use in classroom activities in schools that have purchased this publication.

How much would you give?

- You win a prize at a school fair!
- You have just had your birthday, and had lots of great presents.
- Now you unexpectedly have an extra £100.

Below are some things you could spend your money on.

In pairs, decide how you might spend the £100. Be able to explain why you are using your money like this.

£5 will pay for installing a **water tap** in a village in Nicaragua (AquAid).	£15 will pay for a **goat**, and provide a family with milk to drink and kids to sell on at market.	£99 will buy you a **digital camera**, with a 12x zoom lens.	£86 will pay **a teacher's salary** for two months. Give children in remote areas of **Bangladesh** the chance of an education.
£99 will get you the **Lego Lord of the Rings** 'Battle at Helm's Deep' model.	£16 can buy **20 fruit trees** – these could provide healthy, nutritious fruit for a struggling family in **Nicaragua**.	£80 will buy you a Sony Walkman **MP3 player**, including on-screen lyrics for karaoke!	£71 will pay for a 'winterised' **tent** to provide shelter for a family who has lost their home in a disaster.
£21 will buy **two chickens**. Eggs from these could provide a valuable source of nutrition and extra income.	£10 will buy you a **Spider-Man Hero Mask**.	£15 will pay for **mosquito nets** – these could keep vulnerable children and their families safe while they sleep.	£12 can buy a beehive. **Bees** could provide a valuable source of income for a farmer in **Bolivia**.
£17 will buy you a **One Direction doll**. Collect all 5 for only £85!	£7 will buy a **wormery**. In **India**, worms can help turn wasteland into fertile agricultural land.	£25 would **feed** a refugee family on the Thai-Burma border for a month.	Put your money towards an **iPod Touch** – only £160.

RE Today Services

© 2013 RE Today Services
Permission is granted to photocopy this page for use in classroom activities in schools that have purchased this publication.

What do Christians promise when they welcome a baby?

7–11

For the teacher

In this article, pupils learn from the promises parents make at the baptism of a baby. Then they develop their understanding of symbols and ideas about belonging, and consider the reasons why promises made by mums and dads are important in Christianity and in everyone's lives.

The work might make up four lessons in a unit of work on Christian belief or worship, or a unit of work on prayer, or as part of a unit of work on commitment.

The work is suitable for pupils aged 7–11. There are suitable tasks in each section, to make each activity challenging for the more able pupils.

Becky and George are getting ready for baby Abi's baptism. They will make some promises to God about how they will bring her up.

Essential RE knowledge

This work enables pupils to achieve with regard to the following learning intentions.

They will:

- describe varied practices and ways of life in religions and understand how these connect to beliefs and teachings
- consider the meanings of a baptism, and other forms of religious expression
- reflect on what it means to belong to the Christian community and to the communities they belong to
- respond to the challenges of commitment both in their own lives and within religious traditions
- recognise how commitment is shown in a variety of ways
- consider how and why religious families and communities practise their faith and the contribution this makes to local life.

The following resources are available for subscribers to download from the RE Today website:

- A simple PowerPoint sequence to support the learning in this unit

See: www.retoday.org.uk/supplements

What can children do as a result of this unit?

The following pupil-friendly 'I can' statements describe the learning that may be expected of pupils in the 7–11 age range.

Level	Description of achievement: I can. . .
1	• **use religious words** like 'baptism', 'christening', 'God', 'promise' • **recognise** one thing Christians promise at a baptism • *talk about* what makes a baptism a special occasion.
2	• **identify** two promises that Christians make at a baptism • **recognise a reason** why Christians thank God for a new baby • *respond sensitively* to questions about new life and promises for myself.
3	• **describe** in five steps what happens at a Christian baptism • **use the right words to describe** what difference promises would make to how parents care for their child • **make links between** Christian ideas for welcoming a new baby and my own ideas.
4	• **show understanding** of the way promises have an impact on parents and children • **show that I understand** the idea that God makes promises as well, and these might be trusted by Christian people • **apply the idea** of a 'promise to care' for myself.

20

RE Today Services

Activity 1
Responding to baptism with ideas

Copy the outline on page 22 for pupils to work on in pairs. Aim to get pupils to see the difference between thoughts and feelings, and to think about the promises that are made.

Discuss with the pupils what a mum or dad might promise to a baby when s/he is born. Ask the pupils to work in pairs to come up with some promises.

Show the pupils either a copy of the promises made in the baptism service or

See: www.request.org.uk/main/dowhat/baptism/infant02.htm

Ask the pupils to identify what the vicar and the mum and dad do and don't say at a baptism. Hold up or read out each of the statements at the bottom of the page and ask the children to stand up if they think the question or promise is said, and sit down if the question or promise is not said. After each statement go around and ask the children why they think the question or promise is said or not said.

If you are a member of RE Today, then use the PowerPoint download from the website – it is a high quality photostory of the baptism we feature in this article.

Does Reverend Elaine say . . .	Does Becky promise . . .
Do you believe in God, the Father, Son and Holy Spirit?	I promise to give Abi everything she wants.
Do you turn to Christ?	I promise to help Abi to grow up as a Christian.
Will you love and care for this child?	I promise to pray for Abi.
Will you give this child everything she wants?	I promise to always be a perfect mum.
Will you support this child with your prayers?	I promise to say sorry if I get things wrong.

RE Today Services

© 2013 RE Today Services
Permission is granted to photocopy this page for use in classroom activities in schools that have purchased this publication.

What are Reverend Elaine and Becky thinking, feeling and saying?

I'm Reverend Elaine. Today I'm thinking . . . .

I'm Abi's mum, Becky. Today I am thinking . . . .

Can you use these words as you fill in the bubbles?

Responsibility
Committed
Thankful
Worshipping
Hoping
Symbol of water

Can you use these words as you fill in the bubbles?

Promise
God
Baptism
Christening
Thrilled

I think Becky is feeling . . . .

because . . . .

I think Reverend Elaine is feeling . . . .

because . . . .

22

© 2013 RE Today Services
Permission is granted to photocopy this page for use in classroom activities in schools that have purchased this publication.

RE Today Services

Activity 2
Abi's baptism: what happened and why?

Fill in the missing words from this list:

baptism	shine	belonging	water
Jesus	cross	thankful	life
promises	minister	third	light

Little Abi's mum and dad are Christians, so when she was born they were very _____ to God.

They took Abi to church on Sunday for her _____. It's a sign of _____ to God. Mums and dads make _____ at a baptism, to help the child grow up as a Christian.

There are three symbols at a baptism. The _____ brings the baby to a font and makes the sign of a _____ on her head. It's a reminder of _____

Then the minister baptises the baby by pouring _____ on her head three times. It is a sign of a clean, fresh, new _____.

The _____ symbol is a candle. Jesus said He was the '_____ of the world.' Each Christian – even baby Abi – can _____ for Jesus. Anyone can be kind. Anyone can pray for other people. The candle will be lit again when Abi is confirmed.

Activity 3
Belonging – a talking circle

This excellent discussion strategy is more widely known than used because it takes a little setting up. It is really worth it. The best way to describe it is that it is like speed dating – you move on to a new partner every 90 seconds. If you have 30 children, set 15 chairs in a circle facing outwards, then set the other 15 so that each chair faces one in the inner circle – the picture shows how it works.

Put these questions and prompts on the whiteboard one by one, and tell pupils they have 90 seconds to speak and listen to their partner on that topic. Keep them on their toes by telling them you will ask a few people to say what their partner shared. At the end of the 90 seconds talk on the first prompt, the outside circle all move round one or two seats, and discuss the next question or prompt with their new partner. Keep going like this.

The talking circle gives pupils a chance to speak about RE material that matters to 10 or 15 different partners in an interesting and personal way, all in about 30 minutes. It also sets up writing activities very well.

For pairs to discuss in the talking circle

1. **Belonging – we're all different:** Do you belong to . . . yourself? Your parents? God? Your school? Your town? One country? More than one country? A club, team or group that shares an interest? Tell your partner your 'top three' things to belong to, and why.

2. **New baby:** Tell your partner about a time when you were pleased to meet a new baby. Was there a song, a meal, a present, a card or some other way to make it a special occasion? How is the baby growing up now?

3. **Out to dinner:** Imagine you could take one person from a team, club or group whom you really admire out for lunch. Where would you take them? Why? What would you order? What would you ask? What would you talk about?

4. **Signs of belonging:** In a Christian baby-welcoming ceremony, water, light and the cross are often used to show the baby belongs to God. What symbols or special objects do you have that show where you belong? A prayer mat? A football shirt? Ballet shoes?

5. **Desert island:** Imagine you and all your class were wrecked on a desert island. You survive for the first month! You decide to have a special celebration. What music, food, dance, words, ritual, would you use to celebrate?

6. **Some people believe they belong to God:** What do you think they mean? Would you like to belong to God? Is that the same as belonging to a mosque, church or temple? What do people who belong to God do?

7. **What if . . .:** If you could belong to any team, group, club or company in the whole world, what would you choose and why?

8. **Is it a good idea . . .?** When a baby is welcomed into a church, all the people – maybe hundreds – promise they will help care for the baby. Why might this be a good idea? How do you think the people might keep this promise?

9. **What would you pray?** At a baby's christening, baptism or dedication in the Christian community, the minister prays for the child, and so do the parents. Suggest some good prayers to pray for a new baby. One or two lines each is fine!

10. **Who decides?** Some Christians think a baby can be welcomed as a new Christian. Others think the child should wait and decide for himself if he wants to be a Christian. What do you think?

11. **Promises, promises:** Why is it a good idea to make a promise when you have a baby? Come up with two good reasons between you.

Why do people make marriage vows?

9–11

For the teacher

This series of activities is devised to allow pupils to investigate the reasons people choose to get married, the promises at the centre of a wedding ceremony and the significance of those promises for the rest of the couple's life together.

There are opportunities for the pupils to identify and research answers to their own questions about marriage vows and promises. The unit provides quotes from married couples and information sheets to support learning and stimulate appropriate questioning.

The unit focuses on marriage in Christianity, Judaism and Hinduism with some reference to Islam. The activities can be adapted to focus on different religions and beliefs or reduced so that only two religions form the focus of this activity.

This subject may be a sensitive one for children whose parents have chosen not to get married or where relationships are going through difficulties. Ensure that you are sensitive in the language that you use as you introduce the concepts in this unit of work.

See also

This website has information on wedding suitable for people who hold a variety of beliefs and values. More able pupils may want to use this site for their own research.

See: www.weddingguideuk.com/articles/ceremonies/default.asp

Work in this area fits well with SRE which is often the focus of some work with 9–11 year olds. Further support can be found in *Body & Soul* – a substantial pack of teaching and learning activities to develop self-awareness and an understanding of relationship skills for 9–11s. Activities help pupils to engage their thinking skills and emotional literacy in developing healthy relationships.

See: www.retoday.org.uk

What can children do as a result of this unit?

The following pupil-friendly 'I can' statements describe the learning that may be expected of pupils in the 9–11 age range.

Level	Description of achievement: I can...
3	• **describe** two important aspects of the marriage service for religious people and give one reason why these aspects are important
4	• **make a link between** what people say and do at weddings and what makes a good partnership.
5	• **identify similarities and differences** between marriage vows taken by people from different religions • **apply the ideas** of the importance of wedding vows to promises that I might make now or in the future.
	• **suggest and explain reasons** why many people with a faith want a religious wedding • **explain similarities and differences** between key parts of marriage ceremonies in different religions • **express their own views** and those of others on the challenges and value of marriage.

The following resources are available for subscribers to download from the RE Today website

- A simple PowerPoint sequence to support the learning in this unit
- A copy of the resource sheets on pages 29–31 to download

See: www.retoday.org.uk/supplements

Activity 1
Enquiring into marriage

Cut out each of the four quotations from page 28. Stick each of the quotes into the centre of a piece of A3 paper.

Arrange your class into four groups. You may want to use smaller groups in which case you will need to have two copies of each of the quotes.

Each group starts off with one of the prepared A3 pieces of paper. The papers are then moved in a carousel, with each group doing the new activity with a new quote, reflecting and building on the work of the last group.

Ask pupils to:

a **Read** the quotation. As a group **discuss** and then write underneath the quote the reason/s that this couple chose to marry. Allow about two minutes for this. Move the paper to the next group.

b **Read** the quotation and the response of the previous group. **Discuss** what could be positive about the reason/s that this couple chose to marry. On the left hand side of the quotation write a justification for why they think this is a positive reason to marry. They may have more than one idea.

Allow about five minutes for this. Move the paper to the next group.

c **Read** the quotation and the responses of the previous groups. **Discuss** what could be negative about the reason/s that this couple chose to marry. On the left hand side of the quotation write a justification for why they think this is a negative reason to marry. They may have more than one idea.

Allow about five minutes for this. Move the paper to the last group.

d **Read** the last quotation and the responses of the previous groups. Each group writes three questions they would like to ask the couple about why they chose to get married. Share the finished pieces with the whole class. How do they think the four couples would respond to the class's questions? What are the reasons for getting married?

Now move onto Activity 2.

Activity 2
Enquiring into promises

Arrange your class into groups of six. Give each group the three resource information sheets on pages 29–31. Within each group organise the pupils into pairs. Each pair has one of the resource information sheets to work with. Introduce the activity questions;

What do Christians/ Hindus/Jewish people promise when they get married?

Why do they make these promises?

Ask pupils to:

1 Work in pairs to read their resource information sheet and underline any promises that are made by a couple getting married

2 Identify any further questions they have about the wedding ceremony that they are studying

3 Using the extra information and web links on the resource sheet, research answers to their questions

4 As a pair, prepare a short oral response to the activity questions to share with the rest of their group

5 As a group of six, listen to each other's presentations and identify three similarities and three differences between the promises made when people from different religions get married.

Now move onto Activity 3 on page 27.

Activity 4
Creating a ceremony

This group activity asks pupils to draw together their learning about wedding promises and to think for themselves about what is important in a wedding ceremony and for the rest of a couple's married life together.

Ask pupils to work in groups of four and choose one of the two activities below:

- **Seven steps to a happy marriage:** Have a careful discussion about what seven things will make for a good marriage. Once you have agreed these, take 14 cut-out feet shapes. On seven of the feet write the things you have agreed will make a good marriage. On the other seven feet write a symbolic action that will take place in the marriage ceremony. Each action should match with one of the features of a happy marriage.

OR

- **Creating vows:** Have a careful discussion about what actions, intentions and ways of living will make for a good marriage. Write a new set of wedding vows that a couple could use when getting married. Alternatively you could write this in the form of a 'contract', like the Jewish ketubah, for a couple to sign.

RE Today Services

Activity 3
Report writing

Pupils create an information leaflet titled 'Marriage in different religions' for the local interfaith information centre. The report should:

- be written in the third person
- be written in the present tense
- use technical language
- convey factual information about marriage vows.

The sentence starters below will support pupils in writing their report. For further information on the genre of report writing, **see:** http://bit.ly/VuT4W8

Now move on to Activity 4 on page 26.

Writing a report: marriage in different religions

Choose some of the sentence starters below to help you write your information leaflet.
Choose at least two from each column.

Marriage is an important ceremony for many religious people because . . .	An example of the vows a Christian takes is . . . This vow is important in marriage because . . .	One similarity between promises made in . . . and . . . is . . .	It is interesting that . . .
A key feature of all marriage ceremonies for Christians/ Hindus/ Jewish people is . . .	An example of the promises a Jewish person takes is . . . This promise is important in marriage because . . .	One difference between promises made in . . . and . . . is . . .	Many people who are not religious choose to marry because . . .
Many Christians/ Hindus/ Jewish people think . . .	An example of the steps a Hindu takes in the marriage ceremony are . . . These steps are important in marriage because . . .	Many Christians/ Hindus/ Jewish people find marriage promises helpful because . . .	Many people think that . . .
The marriage ceremony is an ancient ceremony but . . .			

We got married because . . .

> We knew we wanted to have children so we thought it was time to get married. We thought it would be better for the children if their Mum and Dad were married.
>
> Simon and Varsa

> There were 120 people at our wedding, it was a brilliant day that we will always remember. It was a big party but everyone was there because they cared about us.
>
> Natalie and Aaron

> We met at school and were friends for ages before we started going out together. When we had been going out for a while we knew this was for ever and so decided to get married. It was important for us to make our promises to one another before God and our friends and family because when times are hard that is who we will turn to for help.
>
> Ruth and Jacob

> Marriage was really important to us as Muslims because it was something the Prophet did and said others should do too.
>
> Our parents suggested we met and then we found out we got on really well and had loads in common.
>
> We decided we wanted to get married and our families helped us organise the wedding – just the start of our journey together.
>
> Khadija and Ishmael

Resource sheet: marriage promises in Christianity

Extracts from the Church of England Marriage Service

N and N are now to enter this way of life.

They will each give their consent to the other and make solemn vows, and in token of this they will [each] give and receive a ring.

We pray with them that the Holy Spirit will guide and strengthen them, that they may fulfil God's purposes for the whole of their earthly life together.

N, will you take N to be your wife?

Will you love her, comfort her, honour and protect her, and, forsaking all others, be faithful to her as long as you both shall live?

I will

N, will you take N to be your husband?

Will you love him, comfort him, honour and protect him, and, forsaking all others, be faithful to him as long as you both shall live?

I will

Will you, the families and friends of N and N, support and uphold them in their marriage now and in the years to come?

We will

I, N, take you, N,

to be my husband/wife,

to have and to hold

from this day forward;

for better, for worse,

for richer, for poorer,

in sickness and in health,

to love and to cherish,

till death us do part;

Extract from *Common Worship: Pastoral Services*, © The Archbishops Council, 2000, reproduced by permission.

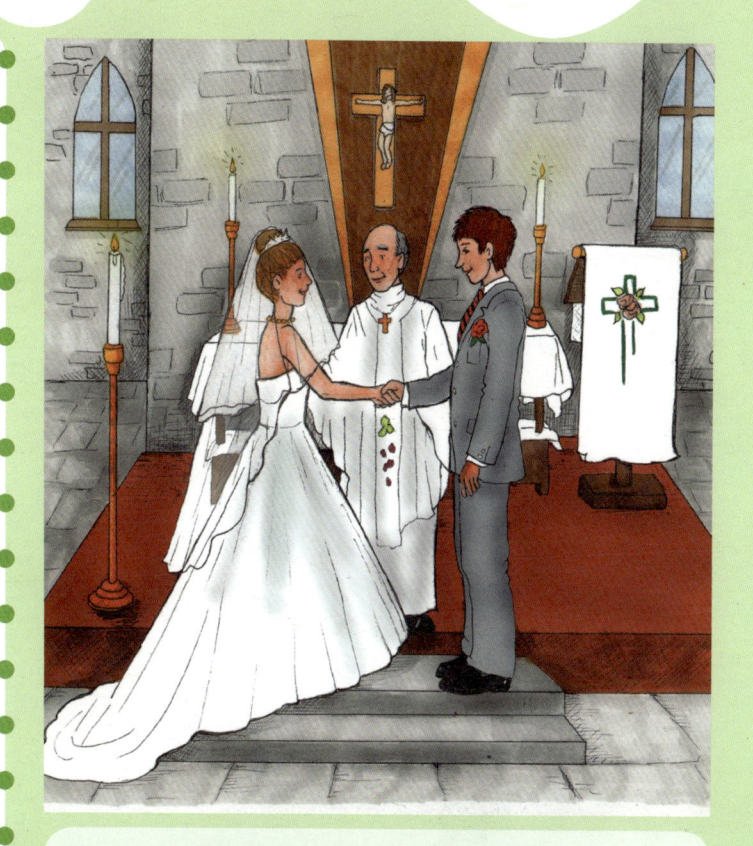

Vows in Christian marriage

When Christians decide to marry they will talk with a minister, vicar or priest in their local chapel or church. Usually the minister will discuss with them the importance of the vows they are going to make to one another.

The vows can't be altered although sometimes couples write a poem, choose a reading or a song to express individual ideas.

For more information on weddings in Christian churches:

see: www.churchofengland.org/weddings-baptisms-funerals/weddings.aspx

www.request.org.uk/main/dowhat/weddings/wedding00.htm

Promises before God

For Christians it is important to make their promises before God. Christians believe that their marriage is a partnership of three – with God there to support them in their marriage.

Prayers in the marriage service express this belief.

Resource sheet: marriage promises in Judaism

The ketubah: a wedding contract for Jewish people

A ketubah is signed before a Jewish wedding by both the bride and the groom. It reminds them of the seriousness of what they are doing and how they must treat one another. Most Jewish people have their ketubah designed specifically for them.

Search under images on the internet for examples of a ketubah.

Chuppah

Traditionally, the chuppah (canopy) consists of a cloth, sheet or a tallit, supported by four poles which are sometimes carried by attendants to the ceremony. A chuppah is symbolic of the home that the wedding couple will build together. There are no walls in this new home, which encourages the couple to follow in the ways of Abraham and Sarah, whose tent was always open to guests.

See: www.refuel.org.uk/jewish-way-of-life/jwol/

Skip the introduction and look under: What we do for 'Time' and then 'Life cycle'.

Exchanging the rings

When Jewish people exchange rings under the chuppah, the man and sometimes the woman speaks these vows.

'With this ring be thou consecrated unto me as my husband according to the law of God and the faith of Israel.'

A sample ketubah

On the first day of the week, the 19th day of the month of Nisan in the year 5771, Jonathan and Miriam entered into a holy covenant as husband and wife, according to the tradition of Moses and Israel, and said each to the other:

I betroth you to me in everlasting faithfulness. In the spirit of Jewish tradition, I will be your loving friend as you are mine. Set me as a seal upon your heart, like the deal upon your hand, for love is stronger than death. And I will cherish you, honour you, uphold and sustain you in all truth and sincerity, in times of joy as well as hardship. I will respect you and the divine image within you. May our hearts be united for ever in faith and hope. Let our home be built on Torah and loving kindness, rich in wisdom and reverence. May we always keep these words in our hearts as a symbol of our eternal commitment to each other: I am my beloved's and my beloved is mine.

This covenant has been witnessed and signed according to the laws and traditions that began with Abraham and Sarah and continued through Moses and the people of Israel. It is valid and binding.

Resource sheet: marriage promises in Hinduism

Saptapadi: seven steps

The most important part of a Hindu wedding is when the bride and groom take seven steps around a holy fire. These seven steps are the vows that they make to one another and the ceremony shows how close they will be to one another in married life. There are different interpretations of what the steps mean. Two different interpretations are given below.

The first step shows that the husband will lead the way.	**We share a drink as a sign of sharing everything.**
The second step means that both families accept the new young person as their own child.	**We share some food as a sign of sharing everything.**
The third step stands for husband and wife accepting and loving each other's families.	**We agree to share our wealth.**
The fourth step is a reminder that children are a gift.	**We hope for good health.**
At the fifth step, we say 'good luck or bad luck, we will be one family'.	**We hope for the gift of children.**
The sixth step reminds us: Happy or sad, bride and groom will share everything.	**We will celebrate all of life's good times.**
The seventh step is to say prayers to the gods and goddesses: may only death end our marriage.	**We pray to God for friendship for each other for ever, to join us together in worship.**

Hindu weddings: a part of life's journey

In Hinduism there are 16 samskaras, events which mark the important parts of life's journey. Not all families follow all of the samskaras.

Marriage is an extremely important samskara.

'For me marriage was the most important day of my life so far. My wife and I are are now united by our beliefs, the seven promises we made, and our love for each other. Our families have come together too.'

Amit

OPENING UP RE: WHAT THE SERIES CONTAINS

The 'Opening up' series aims to:
- **open up** exciting ways of working with beliefs and big questions with 4–11s
- **provide** practical easy-to-use activities to develop good learning in a range of contexts
- **help the RE subject leader** with planning and delivering primary RE within a variety of curriculum approaches to develop the essential skills and concepts in RE

The following chart provides a quick reference to help you locate topics and religions covered in the series.

SL = subject leader

Title	Age	Contents	Religions covered	ISBN
Opening up Values	4–11	Christian values: love – prayer of St Francis; 1 Corinthians 13	Bahá'í Christianity Hindu Islam Judaism Sikh	978-1-905893-30-0
	5–9	Jewish values: hope: Noah; Hanukkah in the concentration camps		
	7–11	Muslim values: peace – saying hello; prayer		
	6–10	Hindu values: being good – code for being good; how to be naughty – drama		
	7–11	Sikh values: equality and service – story 'Dunni Chand'; the langar		
	7–11	Bahá'í values: unity – story 'The Fingers of One Hand'; creating a unity tree Values education in school		
Opening up Islam	4–6	Creative storytelling: stories 'The Woman at the Gates of Makkah' and 'The Boy who Threw Stones at Trees'	Islam	978-1-905893-33-1
	5–11	Allah and Muhammad: music; 99 beautiful names; stories 'Muhammad and the Cat' and 'Muhammad's Wisdom'		
	7–11	Qur'an: why it is special to Muslims; Qur'an similes; story 'The Night of Power'		
	7–11	Pattern and shape in Islam: Islamic gardens		
	7–11	What does it mean to be a Muslim in Britain today?: Five Pillars of Islam (four activities)		
	SL	Representing Islam – 10 tips; Islamophobia		
Opening up Belonging	4–7	Stories of belonging: baptism; aqiqah; shabbat; langar	Christianity Islam Judaism Sikhism	978-1-905893-36-2
	5–7	Who and what do we belong to and how do we show it: similarity and difference; symbols of belonging		
	7–9	Jesus: the 'I am' sayings in John's Gospel		
	7–11	Belonging: places, symbols, festivals, days, clothing, A3 colour poster resource		
	7–11	Belonging through fiction and creative writing: guidance from sacred texts		
	SL	Planning for good RE in a cross-curricular context; four models of RE planning; planning an RE-led cross curricular theme for 5–7s.		
Opening up Hinduism	4–7	Looking and listening activities: persona dolls; puja tray; Raksha Bandhan	Hinduism	978-1-905893-38-6
	6–9	Meaning of Divali – struggling to be good; story 'Prince Ram and Princess Sita'; doing Divali better in RE		
	5–11	Divali progression grid		
	7–9	Enquiry: learning from a murti of the goddess Durga: artefacts; story 'Durga Defeats the Demon Mahishasur'		
	9–11	Beliefs about actions and consequences: five daily duties; reflection diary		
	7–11	Karma; Moksha Chitram game, Hindu sacred text: guided visualisation		
	SL	Representing Hinduism		
Opening up Easter	4–6	Remembering Jesus: sharing the Easter stories; persona dolls; visits and visitors; role play; Easter in church	Christianity	978-1-905893-46-1
	5–7	Using spiritual music: sorrow and joy – emotions in the Easter story		
	7–8	New beginnings – death and resurrection: story 'Grubby Grub'; hot seating; crosses and crucifixes; poetry		
	8–9	What the crucifixion means to Christians: four perspectives; concept of sacrifice		
	9–10	Creating an Easter labyrinth		
	10–11	Easter poetry		
	SL	Planning for progression across the school: progression grid		
Opening up Respect	4–6	Treating people respectfully: Querks; conscience alley; stories 'Sunita the Scavenger' and 'Muhammad and the Thirsty Camel'	All	978-1-905893-51-5
	5–7	Religious diversity: similarity and difference; guess who; matching; story 'David, King of Israel'		
	7–9	Living together in one world: story 'A Week in Yawtown'; responding to dilemmas; A4 visual learning poster		
	8–11	In a community with many differences, how should we live? enquiry – diversity with jelly babies		
	9–11	Planning a multifaith conference; the Values game		

Title	Age	Contents	Religions covered	ISBN
Opening up Judaism	4–6	Shabbat	Judaism	978-1-905893-55-3
	6–7	Synagogue: Jewish artefacts; blessing a baby; story Jewish stories of creation		
	7–9	Rosh Hashanah and Yom Kippur: interview with a child; story 'Jonah and the Big Fish'; conscience alley		
	7–11	Looking after the world: strategies for working with the creation stories in Genesis 1–3		
	9–11	The Holocaust and meaningful RE: Jewish beliefs using poetry, art and quotes from survivors		
	SL	Representing Judaism		
Opening Up Christianity	4–6	Stories about Jesus: visiting storyteller; jigsaw stories; treasure hunt: stories 'Zacchaeus' and 'The Lost Coin'	Christianity	978-1-905893-48-5
	5–6	Caring for living things: 'All things bright and beautiful' song and story; story 'Liquorice and Toffee' (guinea pigs)		
	6–7	What is God like? kenning poems; metaphor match		
	7–11	What do Christians believe and do? Enquiry based on A2 visual learning picture/text		
	7–9	Lent and Advent: the story; card sort; blogs and tweets; visitors		
	9–11	Importance of the Bible: story 'The Lost Son' – disentangling text/translations; graphic Bible; how the Bible is used today		
	SL	Representing Christianity		
Opening Up Creativity	4–6	Why do people have food at special times: story; tasting; lotto; role play	Christianity Islam Judaism	978-1-905893-59-1
	5–7	Asking and answering puzzling questions: six creative activities; story 'The Walnut and the Watermelon' (Islam)		
	7–9	Teaching sacred text creatively: the Adhan; the Shema; Muhammad's farewell sermon; guided visualisation		
	9–11	Creative learning about prayer: prayer cards and images for meditation; letters; diamond nine		
	SL	How to plan an RE day or week in your school; using artefacts creatively		
Opening Up Community	4–6	Buddhism – learning from nature: image cards; matching; using your body	Buddhism Sikhism Humanism	978-1-905893-62-1
	5–7	Sikhism – helping people: sorting, matching, talking; story 'Guru Amar Das and Emperor Akbar'; blogs and tweets; langar;		
	7–9	Sikhism – Baisakhi: mind mapping; mystery; story of formation of the Khalsa		
	9–11	Buddhism – being part of a community: interviews with two Buddhists; co-operation game; active reading; enquiry		
	7–11	Humanism – views and ideas: weddings; code for living; values; sorting and ranking ideas; diamond nine; values auction.		
	SL	Representing: Buddhism; Humanism; Sikhism		
Opening up Thankfulness	4–6	Saying thanks, thank you prayers, thank you poems, the Ten Lepers	Judaism Christianity Islam Hindu	978-1-905893-71-3
	5–7	Welcoming a baby, prayers, poetry, knowledge sharing and a quiz		
	7–9	Harvest celebrations – an enquiry, investigation and group activities interpreting and writing songs, choosing charities and creating a report		
	9–11	Remembrance: original source material on sacrifice and commemoration; cross-curricular work		
	7–11	How do people follow their beliefs and live a generous life? quotes from sacred text, examples of people's actions.		
	SL	Thankfulness in the curriculum, quotes from sacred text		
Opening up Promises	4–6	What and why people promise; human barchart, promise matching, parable of the Two Sons; suggesting meaning in story	Christianity Judaism Hinduism Sikhism	978-1-905893-73-7
	5–7	Noah; story, hot-seating, prayer and poetry; understanding the promises of God		
	7–9	Promise to care; key teachings Christianity and Sikhism, examples of practical caring by use of money and time. What would you do?		
	7–11	Christian infant baptism; promises made, photo resources, talking circle		
	9–11	Marriage: enquiry activities into reasons for marriage and vows made at a wedding, creating a ceremony, literacy link – report writing		
	SL	OURE series overview		

This overview of the 'Opening Up' series is avalable for subscribers to download from our website. For more information on the material in our curriculum publications for the primary classroom, by religion, see http://www.retoday.org.uk/benefit/publications-by-religion/

RE Today Services

The **Opening up RE** series aims to:

- open up exciting ways of working with beliefs and big questions with 4–11s
- provide practical easy-to-use activities to develop good learning in a wide range of contexts
- help the RE **subject leader** with planning and delivering primary RE within a variety of curriculum approaches to develop the essential skills and concepts in RE.

The complete series contains the following titles:

Opening up Values	Opening up Hinduism	Opening up Creativity
Opening up Islam	Opening up Easter	Opening up Community
Opening up Belonging	Opening up Respect	Opening up Thankfulness
Opening up Judaism	Opening up Christianity	Opening up Promises

RE Today Services

ISBN 978-1-905893-73-7

www.retoday.org.uk